# The
# Dried
# Flower
## Arranger's
## Companion

# The Dried Flower

## Arranger's Companion

30 delightfully simple,

stunningly effective

arrangements for all

seasons and occasions.

**KYM HATALA**

CHARTWELL BOOKS, INC.

A QUINTET BOOK

Published by Chartwell Books
A Division of Book Sales, Inc.
110 Enterprise Avenue
Secaucus, New Jersey 07094

This edition produced for sale
in the U.S.A., its territories
and dependencies only.

ISBN 0-7858-0098-0

This book was designed and produced by
Quintet Publishing Limited
6 Blundell Street
London N7 9BH

Creative Director: Richard Dewing
Designer: Ian Hunt
Project Editor: Stefanie Foster
Editor: Lydia Darbyshire
Photography: Paul Forrester and Chas Wilder

Typeset in Great Britain by
Central Southern Typesetters, Eastbourne
Manufactured by Bright Arts (Singapore) Pte Ltd
Printed in Hong Kong by Sing Cheong Printing Co. Ltd.

*Special thanks to Ginger Gilmour*

# Contents

Introduction 6

Drying Methods 7

Materials and Equipment 11

## SPRING

Valentine's Heart 14

Bright and Cheerful 16

Spring Bouquet 18

Mother's Day Posy 20

Art Deco Vase 22

Easter Table Centerpiece 24

Indoor Topiary 26

## SUMMER

At the Seashore 28

Summer Sunshine 29

Dahlia Tree 31

Pretty in Pink 34

Strong Colors 36

Fairy Tale Bride 38

Hydrangea Wreath 40

Fantasy Mirror 41

## FALL

South of France 44

Harvest Wreath 46

Candle Delight 48

Scented Lavender Pot 50

Door Bouquet 52

Gardener's Basket 54

Fantasy Tree 57

## WINTER

Scented Winter Basket 60

Surprise, Surprise! 63

Christmas Wreath 65

Winter Wedding Bouquet 66

Night Light 68

Winter Wreath 70

Everlasting Christmas Tree 72

Free-standing Roses 75

Appendix:

Plants Used in the Projects 77

Drying Methods 78

Index and Acknowledgements 78

# Introduction

*The delightful thing about dried flowers is that they allow us to enjoy the colors and beauty of flowers throughout the year. In the dead of winter, when fresh flowers are difficult to find or expensive and out of reach of many of us, an arrangement of dried flowers offers an attractive and easily accessible alternative.*

There is great satisfaction to be derived from creating something personal and individual. Dried flowers are so versatile that you can create almost any style you wish, from a rustic, country look to dramatic modern displays, and you can use the arrangements to convey your feelings about your home.

Color, form, and texture are the factors that affect the success and most influence the mood of a floral arrangement, and of the three, color is the most important. You can use your flower display to underline or highlight the colors of your curtains, carpets, or other furnishings, and before you begin, you must decide whether you are going to create a multicolored arrangement or work with a range of monochromatic plant materials. Together with the berries, seedheads, moss, and bark you use, the colors with which you work must always coordinate with the colors of the room in which the arrangement is to be placed.

Whether it is expressed in the individual shape of a flower or a plant as a whole, form is as important as any single element of the arrangement. A single form or several forms may be used together – and the secret of successful arranging is to have a happy balance. Too much of one form becomes uninteresting; too many forms can be confusing.

Variety in texture can be achieved by mixing flowers with seedheads or bark or by combining delicate flowers with densely clustered ones. Dried flowers often have a velvety texture; leaves can be shiny or matte; grasses add still another texture. Use these textures to create whatever effect you wish.

When you begin a dried flower arrangement, do not rush. All the materials you will be using are delicate, and many of them will be brittle. Allow yourself plenty of time. You must be patient and work carefully, stopping from time to time to consider the progress of your arrangement and whether it needs more, or even fewer, elements.

The arrangements in this book will show you how simple, easy-to-achieve compositions can look stunning. These projects can be easily adapted to suit your own home and your own preferences, and I hope that you will enjoy making them.

# Drying Methods

*Specialty dried flower stores offer an ever-increasing range of materials, from the everyday to the exotic, in the most wonderful array of colors, sizes, shapes, and textures. There you will find masses of colored statice and baby's breath – essential for large arrangements – as well as seedheads, mosses, and grasses to bring contrast to your display.*

Using bought flowers, however, cannot quite match the satisfaction of using plants that you have picked and dried yourself. You do not need a large garden to provide the materials for an arrangement – herbs, which dry beautifully, can be grown in containers and windowboxes, and a lavender bush takes up little room in a flowerbed. You may have friends who will allow you to gather a few sprays from their gardens, and during walks in the countryside, you will find masses of flowers and leaves that you can dry to add to your collection. You can collect seedheads, nuts and cones as well as grasses from the countryside, and interestingly shaped twigs and pieces of wood will bring an extra dimension to your arrangements.

Drying flowers and foliage is simple. At its most straightforward, it is just a matter of hanging them in a warm, airy place. You can also use desiccants for some delicately colored blooms, while some leaves and bracts respond well to glycerine. More recently, the use of microwave ovens has meant that flowers can be dried in minutes rather than weeks.

Whatever method of drying you use, the flowers and leaves you collect must be as perfect as you can find. Torn leaves and bent petals will be more, not less, obvious when they are dry. Remember, too:

- Flowers should not be quite at the peak of bloom because such flowers often lose their petals during the drying process.

- Do not pick flowers while they are still wet from dew or rain. If necessary, leave flowers to stand in a vase with a little water until the moisture on their petals has dried.

- Before you pick wildflowers, check that they are not of a protected species (your local library should have an up-to-date list) and never pick more than one bloom or spray from each plant so that they can be enjoyed by other people.

Dried flowers are brittle and need careful handling. At first, until you get used to wiring and dealing with fragile material, you will inevitably have piles of unusable petals, flowers, and leaves. Don't throw these away – use them to make potpourri.

**The simplest way of drying flowers is to hang them up in bunches in a dry place.**

## AIR DRYING

The easiest and most traditional method is air drying. You simply hang up your flowers, in loose bunches, in a dry, well-ventilated room away from direct light and leave them. Keep the same kinds of flowers together and try to group the bunches so that they are about the same size – five or six stalks together is ideal. Remove any unwanted leaves, which can lengthen the drying time, and hold the stalks together with rubber bands, which will contract as the stalks shrink. Try to arrange the flowers so that the heads are not packed closely together, so that air can circulate freely. Grasses and stalks of grain should be dried flat: lay them on paper towels on a rack or open shelf. Drying times can range from a few days to several weeks and will depend on the time of the year and the room in which you hang the bunches.

### PLANTS FOR AIR DRYING

Almost any flower can be dried in this way. Try achillea, amaranthus, carnations, helichrysums, goldenrod, lady's mantle, love-in-a-mist, and roses. If you can find stalks of wheat and barley, dry these to add height and texture to your arrangements. The seedheads of honesty, love-in-a-mist, and Chinese lanterns should also be dried in this way.

## WATER DRYING

Although it may sound like a contradiction in terms, some plants dry well if they are left standing in water. Pour about 2 inches of water into a wide-necked container and stand the stems in the water, which will gradually evaporate as the plants dry. Do not leave the plants in the water once they are dry.

### PLANTS TO DRY IN WATER

Among the plants that respond well to being allowed to dry in water are bachelor's buttons, gypsophila (baby's breath), hydrangeas, mimosa, pearly everlasting, and roses.

## PRESERVING IN GLYCERIN

Foliage, bracts, and berries can be preserved in glycerin, which produces wonderfully glossy, supple leaves which contrast beautifully with the matte textures of most dried material. Remove the lower leaves from the stalks before you begin, discard any damaged or discolored leaves, and scrape off any woody bark for about 2 inches from the base. Crush or split the stems. Mix a solution of one part glycerin to two parts very hot water and stand the stems in it, making sure that they are

Several types of flower can be preserved in a glycerine and water solution.

completely submerged to a depth of about 2 inches.

The plants can take up to 10 days to be ready, when they will look darker and feel slightly sticky. You may need to add some more glycerin solution if it is all absorbed before the leaves are completely preserved. You will find that some leaves change color as they absorb the glycerin solution – rosemary and bay leaves turn darker shades of green, and eucalyptus leaves become gunmetal gray. Red berries may mellow to a rich orange, while yellow berries (of holly, for example) turn golden-orange.

### PLANTS TO PRESERVE IN GLYCERIN

The following plants can all be beautifully preserved in glycerin: bay, beech, eucalyptus, baby's breath, laurel, mahonia, mimosa, molucella, viburnum, and yew. Also try rose hips, holly berries, blackberries, and pyracantha berries.

Place the flowers in silica gel crystals, sprinkling crystals over them as well. Keep the

## USING DESICCANTS

Air-dried flowers tend to have that rather faded look that is part of the charm of many arrangements. If you use a desiccant, however, you will find that most flowers will retain their colors beautifully. The most widely used desiccant is silica gel, which you can obtain from craft and dried flower suppliers, department stores, and drugstores. The crystals are white, although you can sometimes obtain blue crystals, which turn pink when the moisture has been absorbed. Although silica gel is not cheap, it can be dried and reused. Alternatives are fine sand, borax, and cornstarch.

Place a layer of your chosen desiccant in the bottom of a container, lay the plant material carefully on the crystals, and carefully and gently cover the flowers with more crystals, making sure that delicate petals are supported. Egg boxes are useful for individual flowers such as roses. The material should be ready for use after about 48

box airtight and the flowers should be dry in two to three days time.

hours, although some larger or particularly fleshy flowers may take longer. Do not leave flowers in silica gel once they are dry or they will become too brittle to use.

---

**PLANTS TO DRY WITH DESICCANTS**

Use a desiccant for individual flowers with delicate petals such as anemones, daffodils, delphiniums, hollyhocks, hydrangea florets, peonies, roses, and tulips.

---

## USING A MICROWAVE

A microwave can dramatically cut the time needed to dry flowers. Microwave ovens vary enormously, however, and you will have to experiment until you find the setting and timing that are appropriate for your own model. In general, use lower settings, because plant material is much less dense than food, and leave the items to stand for 5–10 minutes. Experiment with damaged leaves and flowers until you are confident that your most symmetrical and prettiest blooms will not come out too brittle to use.

In addition to speed, another great advantage of using a microwave is that colors are more likely to stay true, although some shades take on new, unexpected tones – marigolds and calendulas will keep their bright yellows and oranges, while chrysanthemums will take on richer brown hues. White daisies, candytuft, and dogwood stay white, while white delphinium may turn blue. Be especially careful not to "overcook" pale colors with delicate petals, which will quickly look scorched around the edges.

For best results use silica gel; borax and cornmeal, separately or mixed together, can be used but take longer. You will find it easier to dry flower

1. Pour a 1in layer of silica gel into a microwave-safe dish.

2. Trim off all but about 1in of the stem from the flowers.

3. Insert the stems into the silica. Add additional silica if the stems are a little long.

4. Cover the flower tops with silica.

5. Microwave the dish and pour off the silica gel.

6. Carefully brush off silica with a soft brush.

heads than long-stemmed flowers, simply from the point of view of space, although do experiment. Cut off the heads of flowers, leaving a stalk of about 1 inch – experiment with daisies of all kinds, open roses, or carnations – lay them, evenly spaced, on about 1 inch silica gel in the bottom of a microwave-proof dish and carefully cover them with more silica gel, making sure that the flowers are completely covered. Cook for 3–5 minutes, then leave undisturbed for about 10 minutes. Carefully remove the silica gel, which can be dried and reused, using a soft paintbrush to remove any crystals that stick to petals.

Some plant material can be dried in the microwave without any additional desiccant agent, although this does take longer than the silica gel method, and some delicate leaves may lose their shape. Herbs (especially those you may want to use later on in cooking) and unopened rose buds are best suited to this method, although you can also try bachelor's buttons and flower heads composed of masses of tiny blooms such as lady's mantle. Dry the plant material in batches, one kind at a time, laying them, evenly spaced, on paper towels. Cook for 5–8 minutes and leave to stand. Overcooked plant material that becomes too brittle will be perfect in potpourri mixtures.

## PLANTS FOR DRYING IN A MICROWAVE

Among the flowers that can be successfully dried in a microwave are marigolds, chrysanthemums, daisies, baby's breath, strawflowers, hydrangeas, lady's mantle, love-in-a-mist, peonies, primroses, roses, sea lavender, statice, and zinnias. You can also dry herbs – try sage, oregano, rosemary, and the feathery fronds of anise. Grasses, often overlooked by flower arrangers, bring different textures and shapes to arrangements – look out for pampas grass, quaking grass, and even oats and wheat.

## WIRING FLOWER HEADS

If you dry flower heads in silica gel or in the microwave or if you want some especially long-stemmed flowers for a large bouquet, you may need to add stalks. If you are working with plants such as carnations, which have a calyx, use a darning needle to make a hole in the calyx, thread a medium-gauge stub wire through the hole and bend over the top of the wire. Wind the short end of the wire around the longer stem end, then cover the whole wire with brown or green floral tape. Daisy-like flowers, such as helichrysums, can be wired simply by bending a hook in the top of a medium-gauge stub wire. Thread the long end of the wire carefully through the center of the flower so that the hook is caught among the petals in the top of the flower head. Bind as before. If you are using roses or other flowers that still have a short stalk attached to the head, simply attach a stub wire to the stalk with fine florist's wire, then cover the whole stalk with tape.

Wiring a straw flower

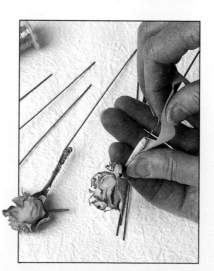

Wiring a dried rose

Wiring hydrangeas

# Materials and Equipment

*You will have spent time and effort thinking about the plant materials you want to use and collecting together the most perfect examples you can find. You can, if you wish, use them quite simply in an attractive container to create a pretty arrangement with no special equipment at all. However, you will be able to extend the range and style of your compositions if you use some stem-holding materials, wires, and tapes.*

Dried stems can be difficult to control, and the use of a plastic foam in which the stems can be held will make your work much easier. Dry foam which is specially made for dried flowers, is available in blocks, small cylinders, spheres, cones, and rings of various sizes. It is usually brown or gray, and it is very light. Do not use the foam that is sold for fresh flowers – if you try to use this in its dry state for dried flowers, you will find that it will crumble and break up and not give you the necessary support that your dried stems will need.

If you have a large container, you can wire two blocks together. If your container is small, the foam can be easily cut with a sharp craft knife.

When you have a large arrangement, you can secure the foam in the bottom of the container with florist's clay and a holder.

If you prefer not to use a plastic foam block, you can do what many arrangers of fresh flowers like to do: simply crumple up some chicken wire into a ball and wedge it into your vase.

## WIRES

Many of the arrangements on the pages that follow use fine binding wire and stub wires. The fine wire, which is sold on small spools, is invaluable for holding together small bunches of flowers or herbs and for holding moss to, say, a wicker wreath. Stub wires,

**The basics you will need for most of the projects in this book – dry foam, knife, scissors, wires, glue sticks and a glue gun.**

which are available in various gauges, have a multitude of uses. You can use them to support weak stems, to lengthen stems for large arrangements, to attach seedheads and cones to wreaths, and to create new stems for flowerheads.

## CONTAINERS

Choosing a suitable container can be as much fun as gathering the various plants that you are going to use. You must always try to select the appropriate container for your arrangement, making sure that it is

A selection of wreaths, rings and bases you can buy or make.

compatible with the colors and style of the room in which it is to be placed. When in doubt, always choose the simplest container. Vases, baskets, pitchers, or bowls can all be used. They can be new or old, made of china or glass, silver or brass, and because you will not be standing the flowers in water, you can also use wood, wicker, or papier-mâché.

Think about the size of the container. It must be appropriate both to the types of flowers you intend to place in it and to its ultimate position in a room. An arrangement intended for the centerpiece of a dining table, for example, must be low enough to allow your guests to see each other across the table.

## TRIMMING

You may decide to add a bow or trimmings to your arrangement. If you can match your curtains or furnishing fabrics so much the better, but remember to keep your decorations simple so that they do not detract from the flowers themselves.

We have used paper ribbon for many of the arrangements. This is available in beautifully subtle colors, which complement the gentle colors of many dried flowers. It is rather fragile, so do take care when you come to open it out. You can also buy gold and silver ribbons, patterned fabric ribbons, and, because your arrangements are dry, the pretty shiny ribbons that are sold to embellish gifts.

## LOOKING AFTER YOUR ARRANGEMENTS

Dried flowers last a long time, but they will not keep forever. You can, however, keep your arrangement fresh and pretty if you remember the following:

- Never place an arrangement in full sun. Nothing is more certain to fade your flowers than direct sunlight.

- Do not place arrangements in rooms in which there is high humidity unless they are protected in some way. Kitchens are rarely good places for dried flowers, and bathrooms can be disastrous.

- Use a soft brush to dust delicate arrangements. If the flowers are fairly robust, you can blow dust off with a hairdryer.

SPRING

# Valentine's Heart

*The plants chosen for this romantic heart, which would be the perfect Valentine's Day gift, are all in shades of red. Red roses are always a favorite, and reindeer moss can be bought already dyed in a variety of colors.*

**YOU WILL NEED**
Spanish moss
Spool of fine florist's wire
14in heart frame
Scissors
Glue gun and sticks
Red and burgundy-colored
  reindeer moss
Red roses
Hydrangea florets
Red paper ribbon
Heavy-gauge stub wires

1 Take the Spanish moss and form it into long sections.

2 Attach it to the frame with florist's wire. When the frame is completely covered, trim the moss so that the surface is neat.

3 Use the glue gun to attach red and burgundy reindeer moss to the covered frame, alternating the colors as you work around the outline.

4 Glue the red roses and hydrangea florets in the spaces around the frame.

5 When the heart is completely covered, make a bow from the red paper ribbon (see Scented Winter Basket, page 60). Push the two ends of the stub wire through the frame and fasten them securely together at the back.

# Bright and Cheerful

*This arrangement of spring flowers in a simple earthenware pitcher will bring a breath of fresh air into your home. The yellow roses form a delightfully bright contrast with the sprays of blue larkspur.*

**YOU WILL NEED**
Pitcher
Plastic foam block
Knife
Bear grass
Scissors
Dark blue larkspur
Yellow roses

1 Use a knife to cut the plastic foam so that it will fit into the pitcher.

2 Place the foam in the pitcher.

3 Insert stalks of bear grass into the foam to give the desired height to your arrangement.

4 Trim the stems of the larkspur to length with scissors and insert them in the pitcher so that they form a fan shape.

5 Add the yellow roses and fill in any gaps with extra stalks of bear grass.

# Spring Bouquet

*This pretty arrangement of spring flowers would be perfect for a spring wedding, and the bouquet can be kept as a long-lasting keepsake of a happy day. Love-in-a-mist is a wonderful flower for dried flower enthusiasts – it is available in various shades of blue, and even white, and the striped seedheads dry well, too.*

1 Lay the sprays of pink larkspur on your work surface to create the overall shape of your arrangement.

**YOU WILL NEED**
Pink and white larkspur
Poppy seedheads
Bear grass
Love-in-a-mist seedheads

Pink roses
Spool of heavy-gauge florist's wire
Scissors
Pink satin ribbon

2 Build up the bouquet in layers of white larkspur and poppies, adding stalks of bear grass as you go.

3 Place the love-in-a-mist and roses on top. Fasten the bouquet together securely with heavy-gauge wire.

4 Trim the stems to an even length.

5 Make a bow with satin ribbon to give your bouquet the perfect finishing touch.

# Mother's Day Posy

*Celebrate Mother's Day with this pretty arrangement of spring flowers. Poppy seedheads come in a wonderful array of shapes and sizes, and they can be used to bring contrasting textures and shapes to your arrangements.*

**YOU WILL NEED**
Yellow roses
Spool of heavy-gauge florist's
  wire

Poppy seedheads
Bear grass
Scissors
White paper ribbon

1 Bunch the roses in groups of three and fasten them together with heavy-gauge wire.

2 Arrange the roses, poppy seedheads, and stalks of bear grass together in a tight bunch, making sure that the bear grass is evenly distributed throughout the bunch.

3 Bind the stalks together with more wire.

4 Trim the stems to an even length.

5 Make a bow from the white paper ribbon, taking care not to make it too large, or it will overpower the flowers rather than complementing them.

6 Fold the tails of the bow in half and cut from the outside corner into the center to give a neat finish.

7 Fasten the bow to the posy.

# Art Deco Vase

*You can use any large vase for this arrangement, but take care to select shades of ribbon that complement or match the color of the vase. Decorating the vase itself with paper ribbon, as we have done in this project, is an ideal way of disguising an unattractive vase or covering up an unsightly chip or crack.*

**YOU WILL NEED**
Large vase
Plastic foam block
Paper ribbon (two colors)
Heavy-gauge stub wire
Poppy seedheads
Larkspur
Dark pink roses
Bear grass

1 Place the plastic foam in the vase.

2 Take one of the paper ribbons and cut two lengths that are double the height of the vase. Twist a length of wire around one end of each length of paper ribbon, leaving enough wire to stick into the plastic foam.

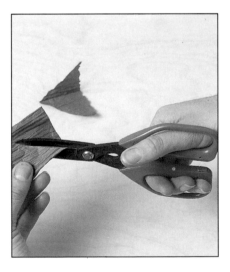

3 Fold the ends of ribbon in half and trim the ends neatly, cutting from the outside corner into the center.

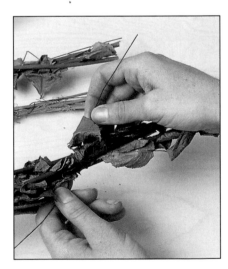

4 Use wire to bind a few poppy seedheads, flowers, and stalks of bear grass into small bunches, leaving enough wire to place in the plastic foam.

5 Arrange the bunches of flowers and foliage in the vase so that they form a fan shape. Put some flowers with shorter stems toward the front to cover the bare stalks.

6 Place the ends of paper ribbon at the back of the arrangement to give it the desired height.

7 Spiral a length of the other color of paper ribbon around the vase.

# Easter Table Centerpiece

*Low compositions such as this are ideal decorations for the dining table because your guests can see each other without having to crane their necks around a tall arrangement. If you wanted to place this arrangement on a side table or coffee table, you could create additional height by using a larger piece of plastic foam and by wiring longer stems onto the flowers, using extra bunches of achillea to fill in any gaps.*

### YOU WILL NEED
Piece of plastic foam
Plastic tray
Bear grass
Blue larkspur
Green amaranthus
Dark red roses

Purple-dyed poppy
   seedheads
Achillea
Spanish moss
Scissors
Heavy-gauge stub wires
3 small terracotta flowerpots

1 Place the plastic foam on a tray. Use bear grass and sprays of larkspur and amaranthus to create the framework for the other flowers.

2 Begin to build up your design, placing the other flowers in the plastic foam. Stop from time to time to assess the overall appearance of the arrangement and to check the height and width.

3 Keep the achillea low in the arrangement to give lift and depth.

4 Fill in any gaps with Spanish moss, and use moss to cover up the edges of the foam and the tray.

5 Pass a length of wire through the hole in the base of one of the pots, and bend it over the rim of the pot to hold it in place. Fill the pot with moss to cover up the wire and insert the end of the wire into the plastic foam.

# Indoor Topiary

*You can use any color of moss you like to make these shapes, which can be used as parts of a larger arrangement. You could, for example, decorate a tall pyramidal shape with colored balls to match your Christmas decorations, or you could add bright yellow everlasting flowers (helichrysums) for an Easter decoration.*

1  Cover a small area of the plastic foam shape with glue and press some moss down. Continue until you have covered the entire shape.

2  Neatly trim the moss to make a smooth surface that follows the shape of the underlying plastic foam.

**YOU WILL NEED**
Assorted sizes and shapes of
    dry plastic foam
Reindeer moss (various
    shades of green)
Glue gun and sticks
Scissors

SUMMER

# At the Seashore

*This bright arrangement of corals and starfish in a sparkling white pitcher would look well in a well-ventilated bathroom. A steamy bathroom is not the ideal place for a dried flower arrangement unless it is protected under a glass dome. Several species of magnolia have large, oval leaves, which can be preserved in glycerin.*

**YOU WILL NEED**
Large pitcher
Plastic foam block
Red magnolia leaves

Heavy-gauge stub wires
Palm leaves
Red and black coral
Starfish

2 Arrange the palm leaves and coral in a fan shape across the pitcher, then insert the wired magnolia leaves, which should fall gracefully across the top rim of the pitcher. When you are happy with the position of the leaves, add the starfish. You may want to add lengths of wire, which could be wrapped around one of the "arms," to hold them in place.

1 Put the plastic foam in the pitcher. Use a large piece of foam that will fit snugly. Push the end of a stub wire through each magnolia leaf, about one-third of the way up from the stem end and near the central vein. Bend the wire so that it lies flat against the leaf, twist the two ends of the wire around the leaf's stem, making sure that there is enough wire to stick into the plastic foam.

# Summer Sunshine

*This is an easy arrangement to make – use it to brighten a dark corner or put it in a north-facing window. Remember that direct sunlight will fade dried flowers. We have used small sunflowers, but you could use any of the daisy-like flowers that dry so well – try helichrysums or immortelles, for example.*

**YOU WILL NEED**

Terracotta flowerpot
Plastic foam block
Knife
Sunflowers (or similar)

Scissors
Green reindeer moss
Glue gun and sticks
Pale blue paper ribbon

1 Trim the plastic foam to fit the pot. Make sure the foam fits tightly into the pot. You may need to attach a holder in the base of the pot.

2 Trim the stems of the flowers so that they are about twice the height of the pot.

3 Arrange the flowers in the plastic foam. Always use an odd number of flowers in arrangements of this kind.

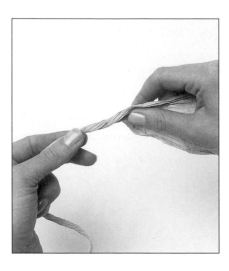

4 Glue the moss around the stalks and over the foam, making sure that it covers the rim of the pot.

5 Open out a length of paper ribbon. Be gentle when you do this because the ribbon tears very easily.

6 Make a bow (see Scented Winter Basket, page 60), taking care that it does not overpower your arrangement.

# Dahlia Tree

*The principle underlying this simple decoration can be applied to a variety of flowers, colors, and sizes, although the sphere of plastic foam must always be in proportion to the flowerpot or container, and you may need to use longer or shorter twigs. If you used a plain cane or stick instead of twigs, you could decorate it with colored ribbon.*

**YOU WILL NEED**
Plastic foam block
Terracotta flowerpot
Knife
Contorted willow twigs
Glue gun and sticks
Green reindeer moss
Plastic foam sphere
Burgundy-colored dahlia heads

1 Cut the plastic foam block so that it fits tightly into the flowerpot.

2 Trim the willow twigs so that they are about 2 inches longer than the pot. We have used three twigs, but you could use five if you preferred.

3 Insert the twigs in the center of the foam, arranging them so that they twine around each other.

4 Glue the twigs in position and leave the glue to dry for about 15 minutes.

6 Push the plastic foam sphere onto the twigs so that they penetrate into the sphere for approximately one-third of its diameter.

7 Turn the arrangement upside down, gently rest the sphere on your work surface and glue the twigs to the sphere. Leave the glue to dry for about 15 minutes.

5 Cover the surface of the plastic foam with moss, gluing it in place and taking care to cover the rim of the pot.

8 Glue the dahlia heads one by one over the surface of the sphere, arranging them neatly and making sure you cover all the foam.

# Pretty in Pink

*This pretty picture frame would make a perfect gift. Amaranthus, which is also known as love-lies-bleeding, bears wonderfully long panicles of tiny red flowers. You can buy green-dyed panicles in specialty shops, and they are worth looking out for as they are such versatile flowers.*

**YOU WILL NEED**
Wooden picture frame
Spanish moss
Glue gun and sticks

Scissors
Green amaranthus
Pink roses

1 Glue moss all the way around the frame.

2 When you are gluing the moss in position, take care that the glue does not drip onto the back of the frame or you will be unable to take off the back to insert a photograph.

3 Leave the glue to dry for about 20 minutes before trimming the moss so that its surface is even and level.

4 Glue the amaranthus panicles in place along the edge of the frame.

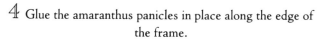

5 Leave the glue to dry before applying the roses in groups of three.

# Strong Colors

*The vibrant colors of achillea, roses, and larkspur make this an ideal arrangement for a room that needs a strong focal point. Baskets are ideal containers for arrangements of summer flowers, and you can buy all kinds of shapes and styles from dried flower and craft stores and from large department stores.*

**YOU WILL NEED**
Plastic foam block
Knife
Basket
Dark green paper ribbon
Scissors
Heavy-gauge stub wires
Achillea
Red roses
Blue larkspur
Bear grass
Glue gun and sticks
Spanish moss

1 Trim the plastic foam and place it in the basket.

2 Cut about six lengths of paper ribbon, each 6 inches long. Twist a stub wire around the end of each, leaving the other end free to insert in the plastic foam.

3 Cut the free end of each length of ribbon into a neat V-shape.

$4$ Insert the flowers in the plastic foam, keeping the achilleas low in the arrangement. Insert the paper leaves and stalks of bear grass between the flowers.

$5$ Glue the moss right around the edge of the basket to hide the plastic foam.

# Fairy Tale Bride

*This headdress is pretty enough for a bride, or you could use it to give an old straw hat a new lease of life. We have used large, eye-catching king proteas, but pink or creamy-yellow roses would look equally lovely.*

**YOU WILL NEED**

Heavy-gauge stub wires
Green florist's tape
Scissors

Spanish moss
Spool of fine florist's wire
Proteas
Glue gun and sticks

1 Bind the stub wires with florist's tape, overlapping the ends under the tape until the joined wire will go comfortably around your head or hat.

2 When the wire is long enough, make a loop in one end and bend the other end back on itself, binding the bent end under neatly with tape, so that you can adjust the length if necessary.

3 Cover the wire with moss, holding it tightly in place with fine florist's wire.

4 Cut off the stalks of the flowers.

5 Glue the flower heads around the circle of moss, keeping the larger ones in the center front and using the smaller flowers and buds around the sides and at the back.

# Hydrangea Wreath

*We have used a thick, rustic-looking braid and pink and cream hydrangea florets, but you could use a grapevine or wicker wreath and different kinds of flowers. Remember to attach a secure wire loop before you glue on the moss so that you can hang up the wreath.*

### YOU WILL NEED
Heavy-gauge stub wires
Wreath
Scissors
Glue gun and sticks
Spanish moss
Hydrangea florets

1 Bend a stub wire in half and twist it to form a loop. Push the ends through the wreath. Bend them back to hold the loop in place.

2 Glue the moss all around the wreath. Be generous with the moss – you can always trim off any excess when you have finished.

3 Glue on hydrangea florets until you have completely covered the moss. Leave the glue to dry for at least 15 minutes before you hang up your wreath.

# Fantasy Mirror

*You can use any mirror with a wooden frame, but you will need to drill two holes in the top edge of the frame through which you can thread the ribbon used to hang it up. The same basic process can, of course, be used to decorate any unattractive frame, and you could select different-colored larkspur and roses – white and pink, for example – so that your revitalized mirror suits your own furnishings.*

**YOU WILL NEED**
Wooden-framed mirror
Black satin ribbon
Glue gun and sticks

Spanish moss
Scissors
Blue larkspur
Yellow roses

1 Thread the ribbon through the holes and make sure it is tied securely.

2 Completely cover the front of the frame with moss.

3 Being careful not to get glue on the back, glue moss along the sides of the frame.

4 Trim the larkspur to length and glue the individual stalks in place, arranging them so that the flowers fan toward the center of the frame.

5 Cut the stalks off the roses and arrange them in groups in the corners of the frame.

6 Glue the roses in position. Do not move the frame for about 20 minutes to allow the glue to dry thoroughly.

# FALL

# South of France

*This arrangement, heavily influenced by the colors and scents of Provence, is a great favorite. Not only is it colorful, but it has a most delightful fragrance, which will permeate any room it stands in. Wire the chili peppers before you begin so that you do not have to stop work in the middle.*

## YOU WILL NEED

| | |
|---|---|
| Plastic foam block | Cinnamon sticks |
| Knife | Poppy seedheads |
| Terracotta flowerpot | Lavender |
| Heavy-gauge stub wire | Brown paper ribbon |
| Chili peppers | Raffia |

1 Cut the plastic foam to size and put it in the flowerpot, making sure it is securely in place. Wire the chili peppers by threading a stub wire through the base of each one and bending the wire back on itself.

2 Twist the shorter end of wire around the longer end so that the chili is held firmly in place. Leave a long enough end to insert into the plastic foam.

3 Arrange the chilies, cinnamon sticks, and poppy seedheads in the center of the plastic foam.

4 Bind the lavender into small bunches and insert the bunches around the edge of the foam. You may need to make a small hole with a knitting needle or piece of wooden dowel.

5 Place a piece of opened-out paper ribbon around the top of the pot, overlapping the ends neatly at the back and gluing them together. Tie a length of raffia around the center of the paper ribbon, fastening it in such a way that you secure a bunch of lavender in the knot.

# Harvest Wreath

*You can use any dried herbs you like in this arrangement, or you could incorporate some dried gourds, which always look attractive. Fasten the herbs into small bunches before you begin so that you do not have to stop. You can use any size wreath, but you should aim to cover it completely with the herbs. This is an ideal decoration for a well-ventilated kitchen.*

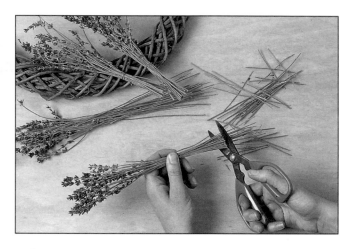

**YOU WILL NEED**

| | |
|---|---|
| Selection of dried herbs – sage, marjoram, oregano, etc. | Scissors |
| | Wreath |
| | 3 corn cobs |
| | Garlic bulbs |
| Spool of heavy-gauge florist's wire | Glue gun and sticks |
| | Raffia |

1 Before you begin, wire small bunches of herbs together and trim the stalks so that they are all approximately the same length.

2 Wire the bunches securely to the wreath, working counterclockwise and winding the wire right around the wreath to hold the stalks firmly in place.

3 When you have covered the wreath with bunches of herbs, wire the three corn cobs to the wreath, placing them at equal distances.

4 Use the glue gun to attach the garlic bulbs.

5 Wind raffia around the wreath, spacing the spirals evenly over the herbs. Bring the ends of the raffia together and tie them in a neat bow.

# Candle Delight

*Although we have used red **Protea** neriifolia flowers, you could adapt this arrangement to suit a different size or style of wall light, and you can, of course, use different colors to coordinate with your own furnishings. Proteas are not easy to grow — they are very tender — but the blooms of many different species are available in most dried flower shops. Look out for the different shapes and colors.*

**YOU WILL NEED**
Bear grass
Blue larkspur
Red proteas

Heavy-gauge stub wires
Scissors
Wall-mounted candle sconce
Orange satin ribbon

1 Arrange the bear grass and larkspur in a fan-shaped bunch on your work surface.

2 Place two or three red proteas on top of the larkspur and grass. Fasten the bunch of flowers tightly together with wire.

3 Trim the ends of the flower stems.

$4$ Use wire to fasten the flowers to the center of the candle sconce.

$5$ Tie the ribbon around the sconce and over the flower stems, and tie it in a neat bow.

# Scented Lavender Pot

*Although we have used fragrant stalks of lavender, you could use any dried herbs –
purple sage would be an attractive alternative.*

## YOU WILL NEED

| | |
|---|---|
| Plastic foam block | Heavy-gauge stub wires |
| Knife | Scissors |
| Terracotta flowerpot | Glue gun and sticks |
| Lavender | Reindoor moss |
| | Raffia |

1 Trim the plastic foam so that it fits tightly into
the flowerpot. Place the foam in the pot. It should come to
about 1 inch below the rim.

2 Separate the lavender stems into small, even-sized
bunches and fasten them together with wire.

3 Trim the bunches so that they are about the same length
and about twice the height of the flowerpot.

4 Insert the bunches of lavender in the plastic foam. You may need to use a knitting needle or piece of wooden dowel to make small holes.

5 Glue moss around the edge of the flowerpot, making sure you cover up all the plastic foam.

6 Leave the glue to dry for about 15 minutes. Wrap a length of raffia around the lavender twice and tie it in a bow.

# Door Bouquet

*You could tie this bouquet to any door inside your home, or in good weather, fasten it to the front door to welcome your guests. If you buy cones from a dried flower supplier, they will probably already have "stems." If you gather and dry your own, add stems with lengths of heavy-gauge wire, which can be covered with green or brown florist's tape.*

**YOU WILL NEED**

| | |
|---|---|
| Sunflowers (or similar flowers) | Poppy seedheads |
| | Cones |
| Achillea | Scissors |
| Celosia | Heavy-gauge stub wires |
| | Red paper ribbon |

1 Arrange the floral material in a fan shape, placing those with the longest stems at the back. Make sure that the colors are distributed evenly throughout your arrangement.

2 Bend a stub wire into a loop, twisting the wire firmly together just below the loop.

3 Wind the free ends of the wire around the stems of the plant material to hold them firmly, making sure that the loop is at the back.

4 Trim the ends of the stems neatly.

5 Make a bow with the paper ribbons, but do not cover the loop, which is used to hang up the arrangement.

# Gardener's Basket

*This is a perfect arrangement for anyone who longs to have a garden of their own – even if you live in a small place and your gardening activities are limited to a windowbox.*

**YOU WILL NEED**
Plastic foam block
Shallow basket with handle
Bear grass
Pink larkspur
Sage
Oregano
Yellow roses
Scissors
Terracotta flowerpot and
    potshards
Gardening tools

1 Place the foam in the center of the basket and insert some stalks of bear grass, spacing them evenly around the edge.

2 Beginning with the flowers with longest stems, start to build up the arrangement.

3 Add the plants with shorter stems, making sure that the colors are distributed evenly throughout and that the plastic foam is completely covered.

4 The roses should be added last. You may need to cut the stems of some of them so that you can achieve a natural effect.

5 Scatter any leaves that have fallen off over the center of the stems to hide any plastic foam that can still be seen.

6 Place the terracotta pot and terracotta potshards on the arrangement.

7 Cut off a few rose heads and place them inside the pot and over the terracotta potshards.

8 Complete the arrangement by placing some gardening tools over the plant stems.

# Fantasy Tree

*You could decorate the moss-covered sphere if you wished. Any of the daisy-like flowers, cut off just behind the head, could be stuck on the moss, or you could insert long-stemmed rose buds through the moss and into the plastic foam. Finish the decoration with a bow of matching satin ribbon. Once you have mastered this technique, there is nothing to stop you from making a three-tier tree.*

**YOU WILL NEED**
Plastic foam block
Knife
Terracotta flowerpot
6 contorted willow twigs
Glue gun and sticks
2 plastic foam spheres, different sizes
Green reindeer moss
Scissors

1 Cut the plastic foam block so that it fits tightly inside the terracotta pot. It should come to about 1 inch below the rim.

2 Take three of the twigs and insert them in the center of the foam block. Glue them in position.

3 Take the large ball and place it on the twigs. Push the ends of the twigs about one-third of the way into the sphere and glue the twigs in place. Leave to dry for about 15 minutes.

4 Insert the three remaining twigs in the large ball and glue in place. Leave to dry before placing the smaller ball on top of the twigs. Turn the arrangement upside down and glue the smaller ball in place.

5 Leave the glue to dry for about 20 minutes.

6 Glue pieces of moss all over both spheres and over the foam in the flowerpot. Make sure that no plastic foam can be seen.

7 Allow the glue to dry before trimming the surfaces neatly, following the contours of the spheres.

WINTER

# Scented Winter Basket

*This sweet-scented basket will cheer up your own home through the cold winter months, or you could make one for a friend – it would be a perfect gift.*

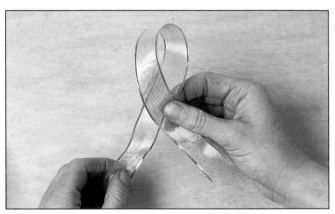

1 Glue three cinnamon sticks together, holding them firmly until the glue has set.

2 Take approximately 6 feet of ribbon and make a loop with one end.

**YOU WILL NEED**

| | |
|---|---|
| Cinnamon sticks | Basket with handle |
| Glue gun and sticks | Lavender |
| Gold ribbon | Red roses |
| Scissors | Beech leaves |
| Spool of fine florist's wire | Assorted seedheads |
| | Potpourri |

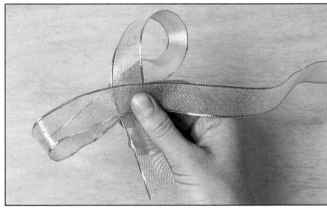

3 Taking care not to twist the ribbon, make another loop over the first.

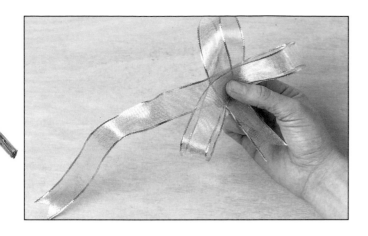

4 Hold the ribbon firmly in one hand and make another loop.

5 Bring the ribbon over the top and make one more loop. The bow should have two short, loose ends and four loops.

6 Still holding the center firmly in one hand, bind the center of the bow tightly with fine wire.

7 Wrap the wire around the sticks of cinnamon you have glued together so that they are held securely at the back of the bow.

8 Use wire to fasten the bow to the bottom of the handle at one side. Bind the handle with ribbon, winding it so that it covers the wicker smoothly.

9 If you wish, make another bow for the other side.

**10** Form the lavender into small bunches. Working in a counterclockwise direction, glue lavender, roses, beech leaves, and seedheads around the edge of the basket.

**11** Fill the basket with potpourri, choosing one that matches or complements the colors of the ribbon and plants around the edge of the basket.

# Surprise, Surprise!

*You can use any container you like for this arrangement. We have used a terracotta-type bowl, but a round basket or porcelain bowl would be equally suitable. If you find that the roses are rather top-heavy, use floral adhesive and a prong to hold the plastic foam firmly in place.*

**YOU WILL NEED**

Floral foam block
Knife
Bowl
Red roses

Green paper ribbon
Scissors
Heavy-gauge stub wires
Glue gun and sticks
Spanish moss

1 Trim the block of plastic foam so that it fits tightly inside the bowl.

2 Insert the roses in the plastic foam. Do not leave the stems so long that they look out of proportion to the height of the bowl.

3 Cut approximately six lengths of paper ribbon, each about 7 inches long. Attach a stub wire to one end of each length and fold the ribbon in half, before cutting the other end at an angle to form a "fish tail."

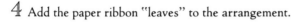

4 Add the paper ribbon "leaves" to the arrangement.

5 Glue moss around the edge of the arrangement, making sure that you cover up all the plastic foam.

# Christmas Wreath

*We have used gold spray paint to give this arrangement a luxurious Christmas look. If you prefer, you could use silver, choosing decorations to match. You must always make sure that you are in a well-ventilated room when you use spray paints – better still, work outside.*

**YOU WILL NEED**
Pine cones
Gold spray paint
Peacock feathers
Scissors
Glue gun and sticks
Wreath
Heavy-gauge stub wires
Christmas decorations
Gold ribbon

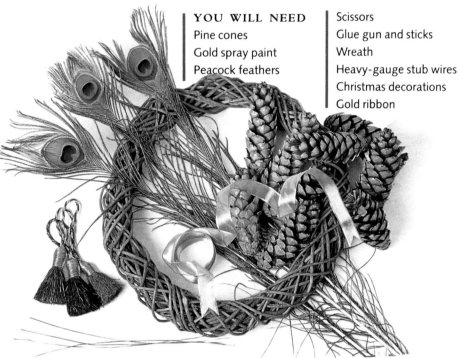

1 Place the pine cones on newspaper and spray them with gold paint. Leave the paint to dry before turning them over to spray the other sides.

2 Trim the peacock feathers so that you have the "eye" sections. Glue the feathers at intervals around the wreath.

3 Wind a stub wire around one end of each pine cone, twisting the ends together to hold the cone firmly.

4 Attach the pine cones around the wreath, alternating them with the peacock feathers.

5 Add the decorations of your choice. We used purple and blue tassels, which contrast well with the gold.

6 Make a bow as described in Scented Winter Basket, page 60, and attach it to the wreath with wire.

# Winter Wedding Bouquet

*This colorful bouquet would be ideal for a winter wedding. Always work on a flat surface to build up bouquets like this – if you try to hold the stems in your hand, you will not be able to make a symmetrical fan shape.*

### YOU WILL NEED

Blue larkspur
Red roses
Green amaranthus
Red celosla

Heavy-gauge florist's wire
Scissors
Gold ribbon

1 Begin with the larkspur and lay them out to form the overall shape of the bouquet.

2 Add the other flowers, the longer ones first, with the shorter ones on top so that the bouquet is full and compact. Use wire to fasten the stems together.

3 Trim the stalks so that they are even. Finish the bouquet with a large bow of gold ribbon.

# Night Light

*We have used white candles for this simple but effective composition, but red or green ones would look equally attractive – remember to choose a ribbon that complements the color of the candles. This arrangement would be an ideal centerpiece for a Christmas dinner table.*

### YOU WILL NEED
Plastic foam block
Knife
Terracotta flowerpot
3 candles

3 large cinnamon sticks
3 long-stemmed red roses
Glue gun and sticks
Reindeer moss
Plaid ribbon

1 Trim the plastic foam so that it fits tightly into the pot. Put the foam into the pot so that it comes to about 1 inch below the rim. If you wish, place a holder in the bottom of the pot to keep the foam secure.

2 Push the candles into the center of the foam. You may need to make holes with a knitting needle or piece of wooden dowel or you may prefer to use candle holders. The candles should not be the same height.

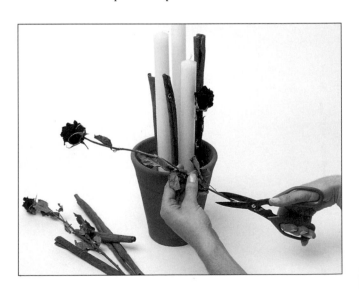

3 Add the cinnamon sticks and red roses, making sure that they are all different heights.

4 Glue the moss around the edge of the pot so that all the plastic foam is hidden.

5 Tie a plaid bow around the bottom of the arrangement, but do not let it overpower the other elements.

# Winter Wreath

*What could be more welcoming on a cold winter's day than the bright, glowing colors of this wreath? Hang it on your front door to greet your guests.*

**YOU WILL NEED**
Wreath
Glue gun and sticks
Spanish moss
Scissors

Red roses
Green amaranthus
Red celosia
Cinnamon sticks
Red satin ribbon

1 Glue moss all over the wreath. Trim off any loose moss so that the surface is smooth.

2 Working in a counterclockwise direction, glue the flowers around the wreath, covering up the stems with the heads of the next ones you add.

3 Glue two or three cinnamon sticks together, leave to dry for about 15 minutes, then glue to the wreath.

4 Wrap the ribbon evenly around the wreath, leaving two long ends.

5 Tie the two ends of the ribbon in a bow.

# Everlasting Christmas Tree

*You could make larger or smaller versions of this Christmas tree, although you must keep the pot and the plastic foam cone in proportion to each other. You can either decorate it as we have done, with exotic seedheads, or with colored glass balls.*

**YOU WILL NEED**
Plastic foam block
Knife
Terracotta flowerpot
Willow twigs
Glue gun and sticks
Plastic foam cone
Green reindeer moss
Potpourri
Assorted seedheads

**1** Cut the plastic foam block so that it fits tightly inside the terracotta pot. Use a holder and adhesive if you wish.

**2** Place three twigs in the center of the plastic foam. The twigs should be about one-quarter of the overall height of the arrangement. Glue the twigs in position and leave to dry for about 15 minutes.

**3** Push the twigs into the bottom of the cone, glue and leave to dry.

4 Glue moss all over the cone.

5 When the glue is dry, trim the moss to give a neat surface.

6 Cover the top of the plastic foam in the pot with glue and scatter on some potpourri.

7 Glue the seedhead decorations, positioning the larger ones at the bottom of the cone.

# Free-Standing Roses

*This effective arrangement is simple to make, and you could use roses of any size and any color. Red roses always work well, however, and this would make a pretty gift, which you could finish with red ribbon instead of raffia to give to someone special.*

**YOU WILL NEED**
Red roses
Raffia
Scissors

1 Divide the roses into three equal bunches and tie them with raffia.

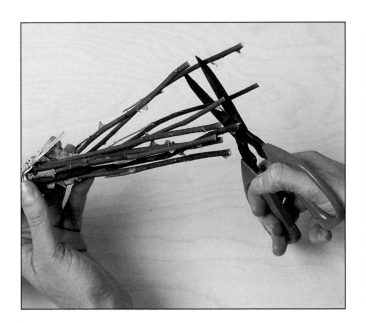

2 Trim the stalks so that all the roses are the same length.

3 Spiral the three bunches together and then tie them with raffia. Finish them with a large bow.

# Appendix:
# Plants Used in the Projects

*The flowers listed below are those that we have used in the arrangements illustrated in this book. They were all bought from dried flower stores, and if you want to use dyed moss and flowers – green amaranthus, for example – you will find a wonderful choice. Proteas are difficult to grow, but all the other plants we have used can be grown in your own backyard – in some areas you can even grow Spanish moss.*

| COMMON NAME(S) | BOTANICAL NAME | PART(S) USED | DRYING METHOD |
|---|---|---|---|
| Achillea | *Achillea filipendulina* | Flowers | Air dry/microwave |
| Amaranthus, Love-lies-bleeding, Tassel flower | *Amaranthus caudatus* | Flowers | Air dry |
| Bear grass | *Dasylirion texanum* | — | Air dry |
| Celosia, Cock's-comb | *Celosia cristata* | Flowers | Air dry |
| Helichrysum, Strawflower | *Helichrysum bracteatum* | Flowers | Air dry/microwave |
| Hydrangea | *Hydrangea macrophylla* | Florets | Water dry/microwave |
| Immortelle | *Xeranthemum annuum* | Flowers | Air dry |
| Larkspur | *Consolida ambigua (Delphinium consolida)* | Flowers | Air dry/desiccant/microwave |
| Lavender | *Lavandula angustifolia* | Flowers | Air dry |
| Love-in-a-mist | *Nigella damascena* | Flowers/seedheads | Air dry/microwave |
| Magnolia | *Magnolia* spp. | Leaves | Glycerine |
| Marjoram | *Origanum majorana* | Leaves | Air dry/microwave |
| Oregano | *Origanum vulgare* | Leaves | Air dry/microwave |
| Poppy | *Papaver orientale* | Seedheads | Air dry |
| Protea, King protea | *Protea cynaroides* | Flowers | Air dry |
| Protea | *Protea neriifolia* | Flowers | Air dry |
| Reindeer moss | *Aladonia rangiferina* | — | Air dry |
| Rose | *Rosa* spp. | Flowers and buds | Air dry/desiccant/microwave |
| Sage | *Salvia officinalis* | Flowers/leaves | Air dry |
| Spanish moss | *Tillandsia usneoides* | — | Air dry |
| Sunflower | *Helianthus annuus* | Flowers | Air dry |

# Drying Methods

*The following plants are just a few of the flowers and leaves that can be dried by the methods indicated. There are no hard and fast rules to follow. Use different methods to dry different plant matrials – you will probably be surprised at how often you are successful.*

| COMMON NAME(S) | BOTANICAL NAME | PART(S) USED | DRYING METHOD |
|---|---|---|---|
| Achillea | *Achillea filipendulina* | Flowers | Air |
| Amaranthus, Love-lies-bleeding, Tassel flower | *Amaranthus caudatus* | Flowers | Air |
| Anemone | *Anemone coronaria* | Flowers | Desiccant |
| Anise | *Pimpinella anisum* | Leaves/seedhead | Microwave/air |
| Baby's breath, Gypsophila | *Gypsophila paniculata* | Flowers | Air/microwave/water/glycerin |
| Bachelor's button | *Centaurea cyanus* | Flowers | Microwave/water |
| Bay, Laurel | *Laurus nobilis* | Leaves | Glycerin |
| Bear grass | *Dasylirion texanum* | — | Air |
| Beech | *Fagus sylvatica* | Leaves | Glycerin |
| Bells of Ireland | *Molucella laevis* | Flowers | Glycerin |
| Candytuft | *Iberis sempervirens* | Flowers | Microwave |
| Carnation, Pink | *Dianthus* spp. | Flowers | Air/microwave |
| Celosia | *Celosia cristata* | Flowers | Air |
| Chinese lantern | *Physalis alkekengi* | Seedhead | Air |
| Chrysanthemum | *Chrysanthemum* spp. | Flowers | Microwave/air |
| Daffodil | *Narcissus* spp. | Flowers | Desiccant |
| Daisy | *Bellis* spp. | Flowers | Microwave/air |
| Delphinium | *Delphinium elatum* | Flowers | Desiccant/microwave |
| Dogwood | *Cornus florida* | Flowers | Microwave |
| Eucalyptus | *Eucalyptus gunnii* | Leaves | Glycerin |
| Goldenrod | *Solidago* spp. | Flowers | Air/microwave |
| Helichrysum, Strawflower, Everlasting flower | *Helichrysum bracteatum* | Flowers | Air/microwave |
| Hollyhock | *Alcea rosea (Althea rosea)* | Flowers | Desiccant |
| Honesty | *Lunaria annua* | Seedhead | Air |

| COMMON NAME(S) | BOTANICAL NAME | PART(S) USED | DRYING METHOD |
|---|---|---|---|
| Hydrangea | *Hydrangea macrophylla* | Florets | Desiccant/water/microwave |
| Immortelle | *Xeranthemum annuum* | Flowers | Air |
| Lady's mantle | *Alchemilla mollis* | Flowers | Air/microwave |
| Larkspur | *Consolida ambigua (Delphinium consolida)* | Flowers | Air/microwave |
| Lavender | *Lavandula angustifolia* | Flowers | Air |
| Love-in-a-mist | *Nigella damascena* | Flowers/seedheads | Air/microwave |
| Magnolia | *Magnolia* spp. | Leaves | Glycerin |
| Mahonia | *Mahonia aquifolium* | Leaves | Glycerin |
| Marigold | *Calendula officinalis* | Flowers | Air/microwave |
| Marjoram | *Origanum majorana* | Leaves | Air |
| Mimosa | *Acacia dealbata* | Flowers | Water/glycerin |
| Oregano | *Origanum vulgare* | Leaves | Microwave/air |
| Pampas grass | *Cortaderia selloana* | Flowers | Air/microwave |
| Pearly everlasting | *Anaphalis margaritacea* | Flowers | Water |
| Peony | *Paeonia* spp. | Flowers | Desiccant/microwave |
| Poppy | *Papaver orientale* | Seedhead | Air |
| Primrose | *Primula* spp. | Flowers | Microwave |
| Quaking grass | *Briza media* | — | Air/microwave |
| Rose | *Rosa* spp. | Flowers | Air/microwave/desiccant/water |
| Rosemary | *Rosmarinus officinalis* | Leaves | Microwave |
| Sage | *Salvia officinalis* | Leaves/flowers | Air/microwave |
| Sea lavender | *Limonium sinuatum* | Flowers | Air/microwave |
| Statice | *Psylliostachys suworowii (statice suworowii)* | Flowers | Air/microwave |
| Sunflower | *Helianthus annuus* | Flowers | Air |
| Tulip | *Tulipa.* spp. | Flowers | Desiccant |
| Viburnum | *Viburnum x bodnantense* | Leaves | Glycerin |
| Yarrow | *Achillea millefolium* | Flowers | Air/glycerin/microwave |
| Yew | *Taxus baccata* | Leaves | Glycerin |
| Zinnia | *Zinnia elegans* | Flowers | Air/microwave |

# Index

**A**

achillea 77, 78
  in Door Bouquet 52–3
  in Easter Table Centerpiece 24–5
  in Strong Colors 36–7
air drying 7
amaranthus (love-lies-bleeding) 77, 78
  in Easter Table Centerpiece 24–5
  in Pretty in Pink 34–5
  in Spring Bouquet 18–19
  in Winter Wedding Bouquet 67
  in Winter Wreath 70–1

**B**

basket arrangements
  Gardener's Basket 54–6
  Scented Winter Basket 60–2
  Strong Colors 36–7
bear grass 77
  in Art Deco Vase 22–3
  in Candle Delight 48–9
  in Easter Table Centerpiece 24–5
  in Mother's Day Posy 20–1
  in Strong Colors 36–37
bouquets & posies
  Door Bouquet 52–3
  Mother's Day Posy 20–1
  Spring Bouquet 18–19
  Winter Wedding Bouquet 67

**C**

candle/lighting arrangements
  Candle Delight 48–9
  Night Light 68–9
celosia (cock's comb) 77, 78
  in Door Bouquet 52–3
  in Winter Wedding Bouquet 67
  in Winter Wreath 70–1
chicken wire 11
chili peppers, in South of France 44–5
Christmas decorations
  Christmas Wreath 65–6
  Everlasting Christmas Tree 72–4
  Indoor Topiary 26
cinnamon sticks
  in Night Light 68–9
  in Scented Winter Basket 60–2
  in South of France 44–5

  in Winter Wreath 70–1
cock's comb, *see celosia*
cones
  in Christmas Wreath 65
  in Door Bouquet 52–3
containers, choosing 11–12
corn cobs, in Harvest Wreath 46–7
corals, in At the Seaside 28–29

**D**

dahlias, in Dahlia Tree 31–3
desiccant, preserving with 8–9
dryng methods 7–10, 78–9

**F**

foam, dry 11
frames
  Fantasy Mirror 41–42
  Pretty in Pink 34–35

**G**

garlic bulbs, in Harvest Wreath 46–47
glycerin, preserving in 8
grasses, drying 7

**H**

hat/headdress trimming 38–39
herbs
  in Gardener's Basket 54–6
  in Harvest Wreath 46–7
Hydrangeas 77, 78
  in Hydrangea Wreath 40
  in Valentine's Heart 14–15

**L**

larkspur 77, 78
  in Art Deco Vase 22–3
  in Bright & Cheerful 16–17
  in Candle Delight 48–9
  in Easter Table Centerpiece 24–5
  in Fantasy Mirror 41–2
  in Gardener's Basket 54–6
  in Spring Bouquet 18–19
  in Strong Colors 36–37
  in Winter Wedding Bouquet 67
lavender 77, 78
  in Scented Lavender Pot 50–1

  in Scented Winter Basket 60–2
  in South of France 44–5
love-lies-bleeding, *see amaranthus*

**M**

magnolia leaves, in At the Seaside 28
microwave, drying in 9–10

**P**

palm leaves, in At the Seaside 28
peacock feathers, in Christmas Wreath 65–6
poppy seedheads 77, 78
  in Art Deco Vase 22–3
  in Door Bouquet 52–3
  in Easter Table Centerpiece 24–5
  in Mother's Day Bouquet 20–1
  in South of France 44–5
  in Spring Bouquet 18–19
proteas 77
  in Candle Delight 48–9
  in Fairy Tale Bride 38–9
protecting & cleaning arrangements 12

**R**

reindeer moss 77
  in Everlasting Christmas Tree 72–4
  in Fantasy Tree 57–8
  in Indoor Topiary 26
  in Night Light 68–9
  in Scented Lavender Pot 50–1
  in Summer Sunshine 29–30
  in Valentine's Heart 14–15
ribbon 12
roses 77, 78
  in Art Deco Vase 22–3
  in Bright & Cheerful 16–17
  in Easter Table Centerpiece 24–5
  in Fantasy Mirror 41–2
  in Free-Standing Roses 75
  in Gardener's Basket 54–6
  in Mother's Day Posy 20
  in Night Light 68–9
  in Pretty in Pink 34–5
  in Scented Winter Basket 60–2
  in Spring Bouquet 18–19

  in Strong Colors 36–7
  in Surprise, Surprise 63–4
  in Valentine's Heart 14–15
  in Winter Wedding Bouquet 67
  in Winter Wreath 70–1

**S**

silica gel, preserving with 8–9
starfish, in At the Seaside 28–9
sunflowers 77, 78
  in Door Bouquet 52–3
  in Summer Sunshine 29–30

**T**

table decorations
  Easter Table Centerpiece 24–5
  Night Light 68–9
trimmings 12

**V**

vase/pot arrangements
  Art Deco Vase 22–24
  At the Seaside 28
  Bright and Cheerful 16–17
  Dahlia Tree 31–2
  Scented Lavender Pot 50–1
  South of France 44–5
  Summer Sunshine 29–30
  Surprise, Surprise 63–4

**W**

water drying 8
wedding arrangements
  Fairy Tale Bride 38–9
  Spring Bouquet 18–19
  Winter Wedding Bouquet 67
willow twigs
  in Dahlia Tree 31–3
  in Everlasting Christmas Tree 72–4
  in Fantasy Tree 57–8
wires 10–11
  wiring flower heads 10
wreaths
  Christmas Wreath 65–6
  Door Bouquet 52–3
  Harvest Wreath 40–1
  Hydrangea Wreath 40–1
  Winter Wreath 70–1